WILD TURKEYS I HAVE KNOWN

JIM JACKSON

ISBN 979-8-88832-379-3 (paperback)
ISBN 979-8-88832-380-9 (digital)

Christian Faith Publishing
832 Park Avenue
Meadville, PA 16335
www.christianfaithpublishing.com

Printed in the United States of America

This book is a tribute to Dr. Robert (Bob) Nelson, who taught us all he has learned relative to wild turkey hunting. Then he took on the difficult task of using the mouth's diaphragm to call in wild toms. Our group swelled from fifteen to twenty and became known as the "Turkey Trott." Thanks, Doc, for all of your time and effort.

He woke up and asked, "What took you so long?"

Let me introduce myself.

I am James (Jim) Jackson.

I've been married for sixty-one years to LuAnn.

I have three children, six grandchildren, and one great-grandchild.

I taught biology for thirty-nine years.

I wrote an outdoor column for a local paper and did some outdoor TV coverage for a local TV station.

I made six half-hour programs.

first met Doc at a Ducks Unlimited meeting, which met regularly at a nearby hospital boardroom. I was not a member of DU, but as the editor of the outdoor section of our local paper, it was an opportunity to meet new people active in the out-of-doors.

After the meeting, Doc came over and introduced himself.

"Have you ever been quail hunting before?" he asked.

"Yes," I replied, "I lived in Missouri for almost two years and had several opportunities. It was even more enjoyable than pheasant hunting. When you bust a covey of these little, fist-sized birds and they have an accurate speed of forty miles per hour in a tenth of a second, there's nothing in the world to compare to it."

"The quail season here opens in November, and I'll call you."

And that is how Doc left it.

In my position as an outdoor writer, I would get numerous invitations like this one, but seldom was there a follow-through.

Well, November came, and I got a call, and the voice at the other end said, "Are you ready to go? This is Doc speaking, and I said I would call."

CHAPTER 2

For more than a decade, the first weekend in November would find Doc quail hunting in the southern states bordering the Missouri River. This area represents the southernmost range of the bobwhite quail in our state. As such, quail populations can experience large fluctuations.

Reflecting back on those hunts, they remain some of my most cherished memories.

How does one put into words the experience of having a covey of quail explode at your feet and then rocket away in a blinding burst of speed?

Doc and I busted numerous coverts during those years, and I never got used to it. It was a real test of my cardiac health.

At some point during those hunts, Doc brought up the subject of wild turkey hunting.

"Have you ever given any thought to wild turkey hunting?" He asked.

"Yes," I replied, "but I have no knowledge of the sport. I do not know where to go and lack the skills and equipment for such a venture."

Doc said, "I know all of the answers to your questions and would be willing to teach you."

As the turkey season approached, my phone rang, and the voice on the other end asked if I was ready to hunt wild turkeys. Of course, true to his word, it was Doc, wondering if I was still interested in the hunt.

"Yes, I'm still interested and anxious to give it a try. When do we leave and what do I need to bring?"

I really had to scramble. Lots of gear would be needed, but being a serious pheasant hunter, there was some overlap. The calls, camouflage clothing, and a proper turkey gun would come later.

Doc had done all of the research, which included getting to know Art, a former GFP employee. Art had written a book on wild turkeys of the Black Hills and was a wealth of information on the subject.

The quest for needed gear has started.

On such short notice, the best gun I could come up with was my old Remington 222 caliber rifle, which was legal in South Dakota. This was shortly replaced by a Savage Model 24, a double-barreled, 222 caliber/20 gauge shotgun barrel. I have continued to use this gun for many years, and it has been responsible for my continued success over the years.

Our first trip was a dismal failure. The wind blew, the snow fell, and it was miserably cold. We saw no sign, nor did we hear a gobble.

Our second trip was off to a much better start. Robbie, Doc's son, had joined us, and the weather was cooperating. We covered lots of ground and did all of the things that wild turkey hunters are supposed to do. Several gobblers "talked" to us but refused to accept what was being offered. The second hunt ended like the first.

"Next year will be better," Doc promised. Next year's hunt was already on the calendar. It's hard to become discouraged in the face of that kind of optimism.

It was back to the drawing board, and I began to acquire additional gear, which included box calls and some peg and slate calls. I've practiced using a mouth-diaphragm call, which I prefer because it takes up little space and produces a wide variety of loud sounds, but is more difficult to use and causes a gag reflex in many users.

And so success would rest upon the third trip. We had been told that the main group of hunters had complained that our earlier group was "high-grading" the area we would be hunting, which would have had a negative effect on their success.

The next year, Rob and I would be joining the larger group, fondly referred to as the Turkey Trott. For me, it was similar to being moved from the kitchen table to the dining room table at Christmastime.

This year, the woods seemed to show more promise because the gobblers were more active. Success now seemed to be a real possibility.

We worked a number of gobblers who refused to come to our calls. They had, by this time, acquired their harem of hens and refused to leave them. Sound thinking!

I found a spot at the head of a steep draw with my back to a big pine, and I began to call. And wonder of wonders, a few hens began to climb toward me. They wouldn't be alone, and sure enough, a mature gobbler followed. The gobbler, always more careful, stayed a discreet distance behind. I pulled the hammer back and pointed at the big bird, who continued to gobble and display

I was afraid the birds would hear my rapidly beating heart, so I didn't move a muscle. The hens were all around me. It was an exciting time.

The gobbler had stopped just out of shotgun range and climbed out of the draw and disappeared into the woods.

He rejoined the hens as they moved past me. I was stunned, being sure he would follow the hens.

"Why didn't you shoot him?" Doc asked.

"You told me to always shoot the bird with the shotgun," I replied. He was displaying behind the hens, which had walked right past me. I believed it was the right choice because he would surely follow the hens.

"You should have popped him with the rifle," he said.

Doc's rules were not always hard and fast and did not always apply.

So, at last, Robbie and I had earned our "wings" and would get to hunt with the "big" guys.

The night before, out came the top maps. At which time, the hunts were laid out, and the hunters were paired up. Since most of the hunters had already paired up, that left Doc, Robbie, and me.

Doc had already picked Ellenbecker Ridge as the spot for our hunt. So we hit the hay because we would be in the woods at the ridiculous hour of 4:00 a.m.!

Leaving the car, we were greeted with gobblers sounding off in every direction. There were three small mountains near us, and a huge flock of turkeys was roosting on top of each one. We had stumbled upon a huge winter roost. Things were looking good for us. Each of the three mountaintops was covered with turkeys. One group would sound off, which would cause the next group to sound off. This continued for the next half hour while we discussed how best to hunt them.

"Doc," I said, "I'm going to sneak up one of these mountains and crawl into the middle of a roost."

He didn't think it could be done, but I insisted on giving it a try. So up the mountain I went, being careful to make as little noise as possible. At first, it was easy because the turkeys were roosted further up and were not disturbed. But now, I've moved into their midst and they have sensed my presence. They began to "putt." By stopping and remaining quiet, they quickly settled down, and I moved into the middle of their roost.

The time had come to pick my spot and wait for the fly down. It was neat to be able to sit and observe what was taking place. I was able to identify every gobbler by their calls and their almost iridescent, blue heads.

The fly down occurred, which sounded like my grandfather's old thrashing machine. There were birds flying everywhere. I almost twisted my head off trying to watch every bird.

It was at this point that I started to call. I didn't know that two gobblers came in behind me. Fortunately, there was a five-foot pine behind me that was giving me enough cover to help get turned around. But my problems continued because the birds were so close that to have shot, at this point, I'd have gotten both. Finally, they separated enough, and I bagged my first wild turkey.

I picked up my gobbler and walked down the hill to where Doc was plucking the two birds.

"I saw a couple of birds heading in my direction. I had enough time to take the scope off my gun, place it in a safe place, and shoot the gobbler going away."

At last, I had bagged my first wild turkey. And I had earned every feather!

CHAPTER 3

A RIGHT CHOICE

After the first couple of hunts with the bolt action 222 caliber, I knew I needed to look for a different gun. And so the hunt begins.

I visited any and all shops that carried guns, which led me to this small, out-of-the-way establishment tucked into an obscure side street. It turned out that the owner/operator was the father of a former student of mine.

We spent a few minutes talking about the son and what was happening in his life before inquiring about my reason for coming in.

"Yes," the owner said. "Think I have what might interest you."

He shuffled several long guns on a wall-mounted rack, and handed me the gun he had in mind. It was love at first sight!

The gun that he handed me was a Savage model 24, which for me was made-to-order for hunting turkeys.

For those who may not recognize the 24, it has two barrels. This particular gun had a 20 gauge, 3 inch barrel topped with a 222 caliber rifle barrel. South Dakota allows turkey hunters to shoot turkeys with a center-fire rifle. So I had found the gun I would use for many years of productive turkey hunting. I was a happy camper. And I had not paid the big bucks that some of my hunting buddies had to shell out. A few had attended a local gun show and looked at some of the German drillings that were offered for sale.

Drillings are handmade from the finest walnut and consist of three barrels, most often two shotgun barrels below and a rifle barrel on top, the caliber of which is often hard to find.

These guns are expensive, the ammo is hard to find, and it takes time to figure out how to use them.

My gun, by comparison, cost very little, took easy to find ammo, was lighter to carry, easy to use, and ended up taking a lot more birds than the drillings.

CHAPTER 4

A CHANCE ENCOUNTER WITH A COUPLE OF LOCAL "RESIDENTS"

As it often happened, I shot my gobbler in the morning of the first day, so there was a need to fill the rest of the day. I heard Mike talking about having a permit to hunt in the park, so I suggested that I tag along. I would do the calling and hopefully get a gobbler to come close enough for Mike to get a shot.

That didn't happen because the gobblers that responded walked away. Obviously, they were henned-up and walked away with their little harems, and it happened a couple more times with the same results. After all this activity, it was break time.

We had been hiking in the woods since first light, so there was a need for rest and food.

Lunch consisted of an orange and a granola bar. A brief nap followed.

After waking up, we found ourselves in the midst of a herd of elk, which was made up of cows and their calves. Remaining still with the wind in our favor, we observed all of the interactions of the herd as they did what elks do when they don't feel threatened.

The wind must have changed. The elk were now at attention and facing our direction. In a blink, they went into stampede mode and made a hasty retreat. The ground shook, and tree branches broke as they retreated to a safer part of the woods.

How many hunters get to share space with an elk herd and get to watch them close up for a good half hour?

Then it was back to the serious task of bagging a mature gobbler. But the woods were quiet. And all of our attempts to get a gobbler to respond failed.

Then, Mike yelled. He had found something for me to see. As I approached, I could see him looking down into a shallow ravine.

We observed a long-dead, mature bighorn ram. It had fallen, broken one of its horns, and died. I marked it on my GPS.

I did return, severed the head, and was met by an awful stench. And every fly in the universe followed me all the way to the car.

Mike had gone ahead, not wishing to have to share that awful smell.

I finally got down to the road and my GPS indicated that a right turn was necessary to reach the car.

As I turned that direction, a young bull buffalo suddenly appeared right in front of me! It had been in a wallow and could not be seen from the road. I could have reached out and touched him!

A quick assessment revealed that there was no avenue of escape. So we stood and observed each other for what seemed to be an eternity. The two of us just stood there, without moving, and stared at each other. Then, without warning, the young bull turned and galloped off!

"What took you so long?" Mike asked, so I took a few minutes to relate my buffalo encounter.

Both of us agreed that it was my good fortune to have escaped without being injured.

Mike was less than happy to have the bighorn skull in the back of his car, but we wrapped it in several layers of plastic and drove to park headquarters. We were unable to find anybody to tell them of our plans for the skull. So it ended up in Sioux Falls. I called our regional office, GFP's. They took care of all that was necessary to get it registered. A hole was drilled into the horn, and a metal peg was driven in that contained all of the important information relative to the skull.

One would think that the story ends here. It didn't.

I got a call from Custer State Park and got criticized for how I handled the bighorn skull. I told the guy on the phone that I worked part-time for GFP at the Outdoor Campus, that we would be using the skull for educational purposes, and that we had properly registered the skull.

We had it cleaned up, and the broken horn was repaired. It now occupies a place on the west wall of the office, where you can observe it the next time you visit the Outdoor Campus.

AMPHITHEATER GOBBLER

So it was decided that we would hunt Elk Mountain in the morning. That was good news for me because Elk Mountain was my favorite spot to hunt. Many of the turkeys I've bagged came from there.

That mountain is located along the Wyoming border and is a good thirty miles long. It rises up several hundred feet from the surrounding prairie, is flat on top, and is surrounded along its edge by ponderosa pine.

Doc went on to say, "Jackson, I'd like you to check out the amphitheater to see if there is any activity there."

The next morning, we made the thirty-mile drive to Elk Mountain, to a spot where we often start our hunts. The truck was driven to a spot where it could not be seen from the road, and we left to begin our hunt. The keys to the truck were placed on top of the front tire for those who finished early and wanted access to the lunch and water left there.

It was still very dark as I worked my way toward the amphitheater. This structure is a natural bowl, up against the mountain, and is surrounded by a ring of trees. Turkeys would fly down from the mountain, gather in the hollow, and begin the breeding cycle. We had encountered turkeys there from time to time, so it was a good idea to check it out.

As I approached, I heard a gobble. It was still pretty dark, and I had several yards to go. A quiet approach was necessary to keep the gobbler from "putting," a response that turkeys make when they sense danger.

I didn't know exactly where he was, and I had to get through the screen of trees and bushes surrounding the amphitheater. I had to get on my hands and knees and crawl. Of course, it was impossible not to make some noise, and the gobbler began to putt. *But* as soon as I stopped, he quit putting.

It should be mentioned here that wild turkeys have a brain the size of a walnut and that most of the brain is given over to the sense of sight. Very little of the brain consists of cerebral tissue, so the turkey has very little memory storage. Once a stimulus occurs, it is noted, but once it stops, it is forgotten, as if it never happened.

Eventually, I worked out of the trees and bushes and could see the amphitheater. And there was the gobbler, sitting on a branch high in a big ponderosa pine.

I sat quietly and waited for the sun to come up, when he would fly down, but there was a good possibility I would not get a shot.

At that time, it was still legal to shoot gobblers off the roost. So I squeezed the trigger, and he fell to the ground.

I rushed over to secure the bird and then carried it back to the truck where it could be cleaned.

While plucking the bird, a voice behind me said, "Mr. Jackson, what are you doing here?" I about jumped out of my skin! We never see other hunters here, and now this one appears out of nowhere, and he happened to be a former student!

"Ray, I might ask you the same question," was my response.

I found out that after graduating from college, he had applied for a job with the forest service, and Elk Mountain was part of the area for which he became responsible!

And now you know the rest of the story!

CHAPTER 6

A TINY VISITOR MAKES MY DAY

The guys had just dropped me off in an area that was new to me. It was a cold day, but the sky was cloudless with no wind. There was a light, powdery snow on the ground. A perfect day for a walk in the woods. Nothing was moving, and it was so quiet that I could hear the beating of my heart.

I was hesitant to move lest I disturb the silence.

Continuing my walk took me uphill to a vantage point where it was possible to view the entire countryside.

Positioned next to a big pine, I surveyed the land around me and enjoyed the quiet beauty of the early spring day.

My attention soon focused upon the busy activity of a pair of mountain bluebirds who were making an abandoned woodpecker hole suitable for their family. They looked to all the world like pieces that had recently fallen from the sky, and I marveled at their beauty.

Then, out of the corner of my eye, a tiny movement caught my attention. You never make sudden movements in turkey woods because turkeys' eyes are designed to receive these images.

Slowly, I turned my head, and much to my surprise, I noted that a tiny chickadee was perched on the barrel of my gun! The image of that tiny bird perched on my gun barrel is now burned in my brain and remains there as a cherished memory.

I did not bag a gobbler that day, but the image of that tiny bird perched on my gun barrel made my day.

I was reminded of something Doc had been saying, hoping that the wisdom it contained would sink in. He said, "The problem with you, young guys, is that unless you shoot a limit, it has not been a successful hunt."

While I did not bag a gobbler that day, I regard it as one of my most favorite hunts.

Well said, Doc.

THE KAMIKAZE GOBBLER

'm sure, by this time, you've gotten the idea that Elk Mountain was usually the chosen destination for our hunts. While this was usually true, Pilger Mountain would be a close second.

Mike and I had chosen Pilger for this trip. Having experienced great success on this mountain over the years, we were looking forward to returning.

We drove to the south end of the mountain and parked in a kind of driveway. A canyon, which runs through part of the canyon, ends here in kind of a meadow. That meadow was covered with turkey droppings. We had hit the "mother load." A quick examination revealed that there were a fair number of gobblers in that bunch. Hen droppings are just a blob, while gobbler's droppings are about the diameter of a little finger and J-shaped.

We began our hunt where the canyon climbs toward the mountain's summit.

Our stalk was slow, careful, and quiet, not wishing to announce our presence. The walk continued, but the turkeys in the area chose not to make a sound.

I don't know why, but I looked up to the edge of the canyon, more than a hundred or so yards above our heads, and there was a nice gobbler looking down on us., I slowly moved my gun into position, pushed the select button to rifle, and squeezed the trigger.

Mike and I were amazed at the gobbler's response. He ducked his head and dived at us, crashing through a cedar tree! We had to fall on our faces to avoid being hit!

Getting to our feet, it was impossible to figure out where he had landed. A good hour was spent looking at every possible spot where he might be hiding.

No drops of blood or shed feathers were found. He had vanished.

We still hunt that area, but when we pass that spot, our thoughts always return to that incident when the "kamikaze" gobbler had us scrambling for cover.

CHAPTER 8

WE EXPERIENCE ANTIQUITY

Rob, who is Doc's son, and I had climbed Elk Mountain to see if we could ambush some gobblers who often fed on the extensive meadow that covered the mountain's top.

There were no turkeys there, and our calls precipitated no responses, so we continued our hike along the fringe of timber at the meadow's edge.

I'm always scanning the country to see what I can see. And, in that country, I look for Native American artifacts that might be just lying on the ground.

We came upon an anthill, which is common in the Hills area. The area around it was cleared, and the cone-shaped hill at its center was constructed with tiny stones of uniform size and shape.

I yelled for Rob to come over and learn a little biology.

"I'm going to show you how ants communicate."

These ants, by the way, were large, red and black, and packed a powerful "punch."

I got a long stick and wiggled it around on the hill.

"Watch what happens, Robbie."

The ants close to the stick became very excited, and this excitement slowly spread to the entire hill.

I told Robbie that these creatures communicate with a chemical called a pheromone. And there are different pheromones for different communications. We watched the anthill for a few more minutes.

Have you noticed that you frequently look but don't see?

Right before my eyes was a beautifully shaped "point," and it had been lying there for many millennia, waiting to be found!

I was anxious for Doc to see my find because he is a self-taught expert on paleopoints. This, I believed, was an atlatl. And Doc verified my identification. He said it was around a thousand years old.

The atlatl is a throwing stick that gives force, speed, distance, and accuracy to a thrown spear. We checked with the resident paleontologist from Augustana College, and he said we were correct on all counts except the point was a minimum of three thousand years old! It was perfect, except for a chip on one corner. But what a find, and I never pass an anthill any more without giving it a once-over.

CHAPTER 9

BLIZZARD AND BROWN TROUT

This story will not be based upon a wild turkey theme. Mike and I had had a successful hunt and were headed back to the motel for lunch, a shower, and a nap. The lunches were great because of the wonderful ham that Doc had shipped from someplace down south. This, along with the salsa and chips, made up a meal that all of us enjoyed.

While munching on the sandwich, the TV was turned on to check on the weather. A nasty front was headed our way and packed a snowfall that could exceed two feet! That front was openly three hours away, so our gear was hastily gathered and packed into the car.

The great thing about hunting in the hills is that there are a lot of things to do if you are not hunting, so our fishing gear was packed into those empty spots.

I suggested that we give French Creek a try as we drove by, and there was still plenty of time before the front hit. Mike agreed and pulled over and stopped. Our gear was assembled quickly. Mike went upstream, and I went downstream to a productive-looking spot.

On the first cast, I got a strike, and on a repeat cast, I hooked a nice fish. The water was stained, and the fish did not surface, so it could not be identified.

I kept the rod's tip high to keep the fish from getting tangled in the roots of a shrub. Mike had come to see what I was fighting, and I heard him say, "What a hog."

After a fifteen-minute tussle, I landed a very large and beautiful brown trout. We admired it, photographed it, and returned it to the water. I think of that fish every time I drive by that spot.

When we got home, I finally got in touch with Doc. He was a little put out by our leaving. But I pointed out that having two more snowed in was not a good idea. He agreed.

CHAPTER 10

THREE DIFFERENT ENCOUNTERS ON THE SAME DAY

Turkey hunters will generally agree that if you have had one encounter per day, it's been a good day. I had better explain that statement.

I paired up with Dick and Russ on a trip back to Elk Mountain. I had never hunted before in the area we were to hunt. This area was accessed through a rancher's front yard. Of course, the rancher expected us to stop for a visit. Then, it was up the mountain to begin our hunt.

We drove to a suitable parking spot and followed the road to where it divided. Russ and Dick went left, and I left them there. They would meet me back at the car at noon. I was left to hunt by myself.

The sun was just coming up on a landscape covered with a light frost. The sunlight refracted from all of those tiny crystals, creating an incredible winter wonderland.

The sun came up, revealing forty miles of old, rugged hills and prairie. The sheer beauty of the area held me spellbound momentarily, causing me to forget the purpose of my coming here.

Every bird in the area now burst into song, and I was a guest in a symphony of indescribable beauty. I just stood there, absorbed by the whole presentation.

In graduate school, we studied ethology, which is the scientific study of animal behavior. We were told that male birds sing to attract mates and to establish territory. After that episode, let me offer a third reason. Those myriads of birds were singing for the sheer joy of living!

All of a sudden, the gobble of a turkey in the woods behind me broke the spell, shocking me back into reality.

I moved toward the gobble, which continued without interruption and was stopped by a dense growth of shrubs, which stopped me momentarily. The gobbler was strutting down the road, well out of range. So I dropped to my knees, crawled into a shallow depression, and found myself in rifle range. I switched to the rifle barrel and moved the rear sight into position. Squeezing the trigger, the shotgun barrel fired! The gobbler shook himself and trotted off. Somehow, the selected was moved to the barrel, and the gobbler escaped.

I continued down the road, hoping for another encounter. And it happened suddenly.

A gobbler was "hot" and coming fast. I did not have time to seek proper cover, so I sat down in the tall grass, got my gun into position, and waited.

A gobbler's head popped up a little to my left, so the gun had to be repositioned. He was looking directly at me, so my movements had to be very slow. The gobbler, being almost in position, pulled in his head and took off. My shot was behind him. You cannot out-react a turkey.

The score was now turkeys–2, Jackson–0.

Discouraged and disgusted, I returned to the car and pouted. When we returned to the motel for lunch, I would have to reveal my lack of hunting skills. Doc would then be forced to cut off my buttons, break my sword, and banish me from Turkey Trott.

Looking at my watch, I discovered that I still had more than two hours left. So off I went in hopes of encountering turkey number three.

A half-hour hike put me in a new country, and I heard a hen yelping that would not stop. There had to be a reason, and I set out to determine why.

I saw a small hill in front of me, and the yelping seemed to come from that direction, heading for that hill. The hill was separated by a small, deep wash. From my backpack, I took a length of rope, tied it to my gun, and lowered it to the bottom of the wash. The gun was pulled up. I climbed out of the wash and started climbing the hill. It was then that I saw the almost white top band of the gobbler's fan. He was displaying it to the hen.

Not wanting to scare him off, I dropped to my knees and began my stalk. Keeping my eye on the fan, I could tell when he was walking away from me, and I would crawl fast, closing the distance between us.

When I had reached shotgun range, I raised to one knee and readied my gun. When he turned around, he saw me, and his beak dropped open. He appeared surprised at my sudden appearance. I squeezed the trigger, and our third encounter was mine. I would keep my buttons and my sword would not be broken!

With the bird in hand, I started back to the car. Lo and behold, Dick and Russ were ahead of me, so I yelped to get their attention. They turned around but failed to spot me. Two more attempts also failed.

My camouflage must have been working better than I thought!

"You guys certainly weren't paying attention to what was going on around you," I said.

"We see you got your turkey," they replied.

"You won't believe how it happened," I said.

CHAPTER 11

I EXPERIENCE POLITICS

taught a course in ecology and tried to give my students actual experience with some of the concepts with which we dealt.

A short distance from my home, there was a state park. So my students and I made several trips to Newton Hills State Park, where they could see first-hand the actual learning concepts in real life.

I became very familiar with the park and its inhabitants. The park supported a healthy population of wild turkeys, and there were deer everywhere. Deer deprivation was quite noticeable.

Alarmed, I called the South Dakota Department of Game, Fish, and Parks and talked with the head man, Jack Merwin. I knew Jack well, having dealt with him on a number of issues over the years. I suggested that the park be open to hunting since it was the money derived from the sale of hunting licenses that purchased the park.

Jack agreed and sent his biologists into the park to make suggestions about future use of the park and its wildlife.

Jack called a few weeks later to inform me that the commission had decided to open the turkey season to the lands outside of the park, and a hundred bowhunting permits were issued for deer hunting within the park.

My oldest son, Chris, applied for one of those turkey permits and was successful. So early in the morning of the turkey opener, we climbed the hill containing the grove where I knew a flock of turkeys preferred to roost.

We got into position and waited for the sun to come up, and there they were on the roost, as I knew they would be.

"Pick one out, line up the sights, holding them a bit high, and squeeze the trigger."

Chris fired at the gobbler, which began to fall, set its wings, flew over our heads, and glided down into the park, where hunting was not allowed.

"Leave the gun with me, go down into the park, and my hand signals will get you to the turkey."

It worked, and Chris claimed his first turkey, and probably the first one to be bagged there in more than fifty years.

It was now my second son's, Jeff's, turn, at the beginning of the next year's turkey season. We used the same tactics I'd used with Chris. At sunrise, we were in position when the sun rose, and we had enough light to shoot.

"Pick that big gobbler right up in front of you, and aim for his head," I told him.

He did and bagged a gobbler that was almost as big as him, and we have a great picture of him posing with that beautiful bird.

I told him to haul his gobbler down the hill to the road and wait there for me. I knew what would happen. A half dozen pickups surrounded Jeff and plied him with questions.

He became an expert and answered all their questions. Jeff will never ever forget that whole experience.

Now it was my turn. The park had been opened up to turkey hunters, but they were limited to shotguns only. The bowhunting permits have also been increased.

I applied for a turkey permit and was successful. At sunrise, I was in the park, watching the sun come up above the trees. It was great watching the forest wake up. But a gobble reminded me of my purpose for being here at such an early hour.

I moved toward the gobble and set up. A few hen yelps had the old boy coming swiftly my way. He paid for his haste. Three Jacksons now have gotten their Newton Hills turkeys.

On my way out to the car, I heard what had to be another hunter trying to make a hen yelp. Keeping well out of shotgun range, I answered. Every time he yelped, I moved and answered. I walked all the way around the hunter before revealing myself. It turned out that the hunter was a former student. When he said that there were turkeys all around him, I never confessed, and he will not know the truth unless he reads this book!

CHAPTER 12

A "BLACK HOLE" EXPERIENCE

My next hunt took me back to Elk Mountain, which involved a long hike up the mountain. I peered through the meadow at the fringe of timber. There, feeding on the edge of the meadow, was a small flock of turkeys, which included one gobbler.

I moved back into the timber and ran about two hundred yards to get into position beyond the flock.

When I looked out, they had turned and were moving in the other direction. I moved back into the timber and ran to get well ahead and wait for the flock to arrive.

A few moments later, the first hen appeared, and then another. Soon the whole flock was feeding in front of me. I knew the gobbler would soon make an appearance. And there he was gobbling, displaying, and showing off to his harem.

His time with them was cut short by the pull of the trigger. He did a backward summersault and did a bit of flopping as I raced to claim him, only to have him fly away.

When relaying the story to Doc, he said, "Jackson, you 'black-holed' that bird."

Gobblers have a thick layer of breast feathers, underneath which is a heavy layer of fat.

My load of copper-plated 5's never got through.

CHAPTER 13

LION, LION

The sun was just rising over the trees around me, and the residents of the woods began to stir. The guys had just dropped me off for a walk that we enjoyed. I was on a hill above a valley overlooking a deserted ranch. The road followed along the edge of Elk Mountain for about three miles. I would walk for a while, set up, and call for half an hour before continuing my walk. It was a technique that had produced gobblers for us over the years.

There had been a light rain as we drove, but it had stopped shortly before our arrival.

I organized my gear, loaded my gun, and started down the hill toward the deserted ranch. The road I was on was unimproved, so after the brief rain, it could be muddy. However, the rain did nothing more than settle the dust.

The dirt on the road was reduced to firm mud.

I moved down the road, checking for turkey tracks and droppings.

There were neither, but there was a large, fresh lion track! It was "smoking" fresh. The lion was aware of my presence, and I would have to be on my guard.

Using a silent, cautious approach, the gobbler sounded off. Moving toward the gobbler, I got close enough to see movement in the meadow. I dropped to my knees and closed the distance separating us.

You have to remember that there was a "hot" gobbler in front of me and a hungry lion somewhere behind me. It was not a pleasant situation.

I crawled in range and bagged a mature gobbler. Very quickly, the gobbler was secured, and I rapidly moved back to where the guys had left me. All the way back, I would stop, turn all the way around, and make sure that the gobbler was not stalking me.

At the top of the hill, my defensive posture could be relaxed since there was open prairie all around my position.

There was time to pick and clean my bird before the guys returned. What a story to tell, and I had pictures to prove it.

JR'S FIRST ENCOUNTER

JR and I rose before 3:00 a.m., dressed, and ate breakfast. He was a new member of our Turkey Trott and was anxious to bag his first turkey.

So here we were at the top of a canyon complex, walking and calling. The woods were silent, and this continued until about noon.

JR said, "Jackson, why not blow that call?"

I did and got a double gobble. That old boy was hot, and he was coming fast. We barely had time to get set when not one, but two gobblers appeared.

One stopped in front of me, but the second walked by me and stopped in front of JR. I waited for him to shoot. Finally, waiting no longer, I fired, and my gobbler got a load of numbers, copper-coated number 5s. Then JR's bird flew right over his head.

"Why didn't you shoot?" I asked.

"I was too busy," he replied.

"Too busy doing what?" was my reply.

"Trying to get my mouth closed. I had dreamed of having a gobbler come in and display himself before me, and there he was. I could only watch. I froze at the controls. When you shot, all reason disappeared," he said.

I walked over to retrieve my bird, and it was gone. The bird had dropped, was flopping around, and I knew it had been hit hard, but it disappeared. A thorough search of the area was fruitless.

A small patch of frothy, red blood was found, indicating that his lungs had been damaged. With his last breath, he must have spread his wings and glided to the next ridge before dying.

Wild turkeys are tenacious for life and dislike being around when death makes an appearance. JR would score on another day.

CHAPTER 15

I RODE A GOBBLER AND SURVIVED!

There was a movement afoot to make it more difficult for me to get my bird. Dick and Russ would be my partners, but we would hunt different areas. They dropped me off near the entrance of a canyon we used to hunt a few years ago.

After leaving me, they mentioned where they would hunt but would return to pick me up at noon.

It was really dark, and it took a while for my eyes to get accustomed to the dark. Continuing my hike, I reached the woods and started to call. Immediately, a hen answered and kept calling. I let her move past me before setting up. She circled me and kept calling. Then a gobbler decided to become involved.

I waited until the hen had moved past me, then found a suitable spot from which the gobbler could be called. He wouldn't move even though he continued to answer every time I called.

That gobbler displayed and patrolled back and forth on a log, about thirty-five yards away. I waited until he reached the end of the log and turned around, then I fired.

He fell back over the log, and I ran to secure him. The gobbler started to rise to his feet, so I jumped on his back. If I could have stayed there for eight seconds, it would have been scored as a "ride," but he died shortly after I jumped on him.

Then it was back to the road, where the bird was plucked and cleaned. That whole episode took very little time, and I still had more than three hours until the guys came to pick me up. So I decided to hike to where they were hunting. It turned out to be several miles, but I was committed. Fortunately, a Jeep with a hunter stopped and asked where I was going. I told him about the two hunters who planned to pick me up. He had seen their vehicle and would take me there. Russ had told me there was a key wired under the car. I looked that car over twice and never found it. I was dying of thirst, and there was cold water in the cooler that could not be reached.

They finally arrived to experience two surprises. I had found them, and I had a turkey!

A TURKEY AT MORE THAN NINETY-FIVE YARDS WITH A SHOTGUN!

Dick and I had been hunting in the park all morning with no success. So we returned to his car.

He began to put things away when I shouted, "Turkeys!"

Dick rapidly threw gear aside to get to his gun. He found it as a flock of turkeys ran by. He removed the case and chambered the shells. By this time, the turkeys were climbing the hill a long ways from where we were standing.

"Can you hit him from here?" I asked.

"We'll find out," he replied, and shot. That gobbler flipped over backward and was stone-cold dead!

Just at that time, JR happened by, saw the whole episode, stopped, and paced off into the distance.

"Dick, that shot was made at ninety-five paces and with a shotgun," JR said.

When we cleaned the bird, a single pellet through the eye was all that could be found. It was a remarkable shot, and we still talk about it.

CHAPTER 17

THE LOST IS FOUND

Mike and I had already made that early morning hunt and had returned empty. Lunch was followed by a shower and a much needed nap.

My nap was interrupted when Mike suggested we go for a drive.

After all, we had come to hunt turkeys, and taking a nap was not getting us any closer to that goal.

Our drive took us through the village of Pringle, and soon we were heading north. At a small cemetery, the road led us to a quaint ranch surrounded by a large pasture. A small herd of cattle were grazing contentedly. It was the picture of peace and tranquility. But what really caught our attention was the large flock of turkeys feeding out there. The flock included three gobblers that were trying to impress the hens of the flock.

After watching the flock, we moved on and found a good spot to set up and do some calling.

A gobbler answered and started toward us but stopped and refused to come closer. Then, for reasons known only to turkeys, he moved off and did not answer our calls.

"I'm moving on," I told Mike, but he decided to remain in the hope of bringing back the gobbler.

Continuing my walk, I came to an area where they had been blasting for rose quartz. That's how they get those big chunks sold to tourists.

Moving on required a steep climb to get to the next ridge. Near the top, a turkey head appeared, followed quickly by another. It was a gobbler.

I crawled closer, dropping to my knees. The hen flew, and the gobbler followed. The gun came up, and I shot the gobbler going away. He dropped, shedding feathers as he rolled.

When I arrived at the spot where I thought he fell, he had disappeared! A thorough search produced nothing. Then, remembering that the bird had shed a lot of feathers, it became apparent that the wrong area was being searched.

Returning to the ridge where the spent shell was found, I followed the trail of feathers to the fallen bird. Rolling in the shed feathers, the bird

I picked up my turkey, returned to the car, and found Mike taking a nap.

CHAPTER 18

THE POSTAL SERVICE DELIVERS

Doc, Rob, and I were making our way to an afternoon hunt near where I got my first turkey. I was set up and had six or eight jakes trotting by. I'd have rather shot a mature gobbler, but a bird in the hand.

Since I had my bird, Doc suggested that I get the car and meet him and Rob at the bottom of the mountain.

On my way to the car, it seemed like a good idea to blow my turkey call. I got an immediate answer, and that gobbler was coming fast. Then he was standing in front of me and had me spotted.

Remaining absolutely quiet, he failed to identify me. He must have made three or four trips around me, and I considered catching him if he got any closer. This idea was rejected as a bad one.

By standing up, he saw what I was, and he shifted into four-wheel drive and disappeared.

Arriving at the road, a problem presented itself. Do I turn right or left? These were the days before GPS, so right seemed the correct choice. Three miles later, it was clear that the right turn was the wrong choice.

Then, just like in the movies, the "cavalry" appeared in the form of a rural mail carrier!

He stopped, and I asked if he had seen our parked car.

"Yes," he said, "about five miles east of us."

And I had been walking west!

"Would it be possible to get a ride?" I asked.

"I'm not supposed to give rides to unauthorized people," he replied.

"I won't tell if you don't," I said.

He allowed me to get in and took me to the parked car.

Doc and Rob were waiting for me at the bottom of the mountain, and we talked about what had happened to me.

My encounter with the gobbler really set him off.

"We had a gobbler coming, and you called him away," said Doc.

"No way," I replied. "That bird came from the wrong direction."

But Doc was never satisfied with that explanation.

CHAPTER 19

THAT'S A LOT OF BS

Chris and I always look forward to the coming of fall. It's the beginning of the hunting season. That's a given. Part of this fondness is that on the calendar, a few days are circled, marking the opening of the fall turkey season.

Chris and I arose before sunrise and drove to a ranch built on the bluffs overlooking the Missouri River. It's a beautiful spot with the trees dressed in their fall finery.

We arrived at sunrise and were met by Dave, who just happens to run the place. Out there by himself, he gets few visitors, so we visited for the better part of an hour.

Then it was time for some serious turkey hunting. Having hunted there before, we headed for a country that had produced before. That plan did not fail us. In the first hour, two gobblers had been ambushed. Now, what do you do for the rest of the time?

"Let's go up on top and hunt grouse," I suggested. Chris agreed, and up we went.

"You take my truck and drive to the other side of the ranch, and I'll walk toward you."

Walking along the bluffs is a good way to hunt grouse. They tuck in under the edge of the bluff, facing down. When flushed, they fly down to the cover below.

I started my walk toward Chris and noticed a big clump of little bluestem grass, a particular favorite of mine. Not wishing to damage it, I stepped over. Bad mistake. There was a fresh "cow pie" (manure) on the other side. My feet suddenly rose above my head. I landed in the "pie," sliding from ankle to hip. Taking off my pants, Chris came over to see what the matter was.

"I will not get into my truck with these pants. I'll hunt in my shorts if necessary."

Chris had a pair of "greenies" from work and saved my day.

I've often been accused of being full of *it* but never covered by *it*!

CHAPTER 20

HURRAY FOR TV

My writing job had dried up, so TV seemed like a good option. I put together some ideas and presented them to the editor of our local TV station. He liked them, and a team was put together.

After a few weeks, we set up several programs. Several scripts were written, and gear was gathered.

Only one program dealt with turkeys. We got an invitation from a businessman in Rapid City who ran a commercial turkey hunting operation. He wanted us to come and film it.

For this hunt, we would be using guns made by Valmet. The quality of these guns was excellent.

They are built on an over-under design with interchangeable barrels. You can order them with any arrangement of gauges or calibers. I chose to have a 12-gauge magnum paired with a .222 cal. rifle barrel.

They put us up in a motel, fed us, and provided a guide. Our day started at 4:00 a.m., when breakfast was served, and ended around 4:00 p.m., when supper was served.

We would walk, call, and try to put a gobbler to bed. The next morning, our job was to wait for him to fly down, call him in, and shoot him.

The businessman, who we'll call John, acted as our guide the first day. We hunted on his land, and he pointed out the deep ruts that Custer's troops had made when they came on a photographic run more than a century ago.

Almost at that spot, I ambushed a nice jake.

Failing to put a gobbler to bed, we continued to walk and call. John stopped and called. Across a canyon, at the base of a tall mountain, he got an answer. More than a mile away, at the top of that mountain, a gobbler appeared and started toward us.

Now I'm pretty good with mouth calls, but John was an artist. That bird came down the mountain, crossed a meadow, flew across a stream, and climbed the mountain where we stood. A member of our team shot, and we were finished.

The next morning, as we were packing to leave, I asked about the Styrofoam turkey decoy sitting above the fireplace.

"I thought you would never ask," he said. "One of our clients is responsible for that. We had put a gobbler to bed and had set up the next morning and waited for him to fly down. We called, he came on a dead run and mounted the decoy. Our client fired and blew the gobbler off the decoy. The gobbler ran off unharmed, shaking his head!"

I could imagine him saying to himself, *It just ain't worth it!*

We shot enough tape for a half-hour program, which the station still maintains in its film library.

TWO GOBBLER ARE BETTER THAN ONE

know that by now you've gotten the idea that the only place I hunted was Elk Mountain. And the only hunters with whom I hunted were members of our Turkey Trott. Not true.

Lee is my very good friend who is a retired heart surgeon. Like me, he was a serious turkey hunter, but he hunted with his group in another part of the hills.

One weekend, he invited me to hunt with him, which I eagerly accepted. As a matter of fact, I hunted with him on a number of occasions after that, and one trip stands out in my mind.

We were set up in one of his favorite spots, calling and receiving answers. Our spot was not the best. A small flock walked by us, and we didn't get a shot.

"Now I'm going to show you how I hunt turkeys," I said. And I followed behind them, being careful to remain hidden in the timber.

The turkeys got to the end of the meadow, turned around, and started back toward me. Soon, they were in range. I picked out a couple, squeezed the trigger, and bagged a couple of gobblers.

"Did you get one?" Lee asked.

"No, I've got two," I replied.

Let me hasten to tell you, where we were hunting, hunters could take two gobblers.

CHAPTER 22

ADIOS TURKEY HUNTING

Time passed all too quickly, and members of the Turkey Trott became too old or died. For a few years, none returned to do the hunting.

Then Mike called to tell me that he and JR wanted to renew the hunt and asked if I was interested. There would be no early morning hunts and the hikes that went with them.

We did manage to get three or four gobblers, either by ambushing or calling them in.

Finally, on what would be our last hunt, Mike let me off at a good looking spot. He would return in a couple of hours.

I climbed to a vantage spot with a great view of the surrounding area and set up.

On the first call, I got an answer, but it was quite far away. Another call and it was closer. Then all of a sudden, there were two turkeys, and they were close enough to almost touch. Their breast feathers had a light-colored edge, so they were hens. However, they acted like gobblers, so when one went into a full display, I shot *it*.

There was no beard, nor were there any spurs. An internal exam produced no gonads either. I had shot what could be called a hermaphrodite. Could he have been classified as a transgender?

What a way to end turkey hunting, but the memories live on.

At the conclusion of this book, I'd like to give credit to my Maker for the opportunities he gave me and the ability to communicate them to you, the public. Thank you, and God bless.

James Jackson has been an avid hunter, sportsman, and lover of God's creation all his life. Hunting turkeys has given him many wonderful pleasant hours of enjoyment with fellow turkey hunters over many years.

His main occupation for thirty-nine years was teaching high school science in the Sioux Falls Public Schools. For a period of two years, he was released afternoons to serve as the education liaison in the development of the facility called "The Outdoor Campus." The purpose of this amazing place was a vision of the Game Fish and Parks leadership who understood the potential of such a place—a place that promotes an appreciation for outdoor activities and love of nature. They state "The purpose of the Outdoor Campus is to provide hands-on experiences in hunting, fishing, outdoor skills, and conservation science." James worked with a very capable and amazing woman whose name is Thea Ryan to "get it going." He and Thea had the job of planning the details of how it could best be utilized for the enjoyment and educational programming and carrying out the many details involved in that. The Outdoor Campus has now been in existence for over twenty years. It continues to be a place families enjoy the experiences it provides.

It is located in Sioux Falls, South Dakota, at Sertoma Park.